by Iain Gray

Lang**Syne**

PUBLISHING

WRITING *to* REMEMBER

Lang**Syne**

PUBLISHING

WRITING *to* REMEMBER

79 Main Street, Newtongrange,
Midlothian EH22 4NA
Tel: 0131 344 0414   Fax: 0845 075 6085
E-mail: info@lang-syne.co.uk
www.langsyneshop.co.uk

Design by Dorothy Meikle
Printed by Printwell Ltd
© Lang Syne Publishers Ltd 2016

ISBN 978-1-85217-213-8

Fleming

LET THE DEED SHAW

Echoes of a far distant past
can still be found in most names

Chapter one:

Origins of Scottish surnames

by George Forbes

It all began with the Normans.

For it was they who introduced surnames into common usage more than a thousand years ago, initially based on the title of their estates, local villages and chateaux in France to distinguish and identify these landholdings, usually acquired at the point of a bloodstained sword.

Such grand descriptions also helped enhance the prestige of these arrogant warlords and generally glorify their lofty positions high above the humble serfs slaving away below in the pecking order who only had single names, often with Biblical connotations as in Pierre and Jacques.

The only descriptive distinctions among this peasantry concerned their occupations, like Pierre the swineherd or Jacques the ferryman.

The Normans themselves were originally Vikings (or Northmen) who raided, colonised and eventually settled down around the French coastline.

They had sailed up the Seine in their longboats in 900AD under their ferocious leader Rollo and ruled the roost in north east France before sailing over to conquer England, bringing their relatively new tradition of having surnames with them.

It took another hundred years for the Normans to percolate northwards and surnames did not begin to appear in Scotland until the thirteenth century.

These adventurous knights brought an aura of chivalry with them and it was said no damsel of any distinction would marry a man unless he had at least two names.

The family names included that of Scotland's great hero Robert De Brus and his compatriots were warriors from families like the De Morevils, De Umphravils, De Berkelais, De Quincis, De Viponts and De Vaux.

As the knights settled the boundaries of their vast estates, they took territorial names, as in Hamilton, Moray, Crawford, Cunningham, Dunbar, Ross, Wemyss, Dundas, Galloway, Renfrew, Greenhill, Hazelwood, Sandylands and Church-hill.

Other names, though not with any obvious geographical or topographical features, nevertheless derived from ancient parishes like Douglas, Forbes, Dalyell and Guthrie.

Other surnames were coined in connection with occupations, castles or legendary deeds.

Stuart originated in the word steward, a prestigious post which was an integral part of any large medieval household. The same applied to Cooks, Chamberlains, Constables and Porters.

Borders towns and forts – needed in areas like the Debateable Lands which were constantly fought over by feuding local families – had their own distinctive names; and it was often from them that the resident groups took their communal titles, as in the Grahams of Annandale, the Elliots and Armstrongs of the East Marches, the Scotts and Kerrs of Teviotdale and Eskdale.

Even physical attributes crept into surnames, as in Small, Little and More (the latter being 'beg' in Gaelic), Long or Lang, Stark, Stout, Strong or Strang and even Jolly.

Mieklejohns would have had the strength of several men, while Littlejohn was named after the legendary sidekick of Robin Hood.

Colours got into the act with Black, White, Grey, Brown and Green (Red developed into Reid, Ruddy or Ruddiman). Blue was rare and nobody ever wanted to be associated with yellow.

Pompous worthies took the name Wiseman, Goodman and Goodall.

Words intimating the sons of leading figures were soon affiliated into the language as in Johnson, Adamson, Richardson and Thomson, while the Norman equivalent of Fitz (from the French-Latin 'filius' meaning 'son') cropped up in Fitzmaurice and Fitzgerald.

The prefix 'Mac' was 'son of' in Gaelic and clans often originated with occupations – as in

MacNab being sons of the Abbot, MacPherson and MacVicar being sons of the minister and MacIntosh being sons of the chief.

The church's influence could be found in the names Kirk, Clerk, Clarke, Bishop, Friar and Monk. Proctor came from a church official, Singer and Sangster from choristers, Gilchrist and Gillies from Christ's servant, Mitchell, Gilmory and Gilmour from servants of St Michael and Mary, Malcolm from a servant of Columba and Gillespie from a bishop's servant.

The rudimentary medical profession was represented by Barber (a trade which also once included dentistry and surgery) as well as Leech or Leitch.

Businessmen produced Merchants, Mercers, Monypennies, Chapmans, Sellers and Scales, while down at the old village watermill the names that cropped up included Miller, Walker and Fuller.

Other self explanatory trades included Coopers, Brands, Barkers, Tanners, Skinners, Brewsters and Brewers, Tailors, Saddlers, Wrights,

Cartwrights, Smiths, Harpers, Joiners, Sawyers, Masons and Plumbers.

Even the scenery was utilised as in Craig, Moor, Hill, Glen, Wood and Forrest.

Rank, whether high or low, took its place with Laird, Barron, Knight, Tennant, Farmer, Husband, Granger, Grieve, Shepherd, Shearer and Fletcher.

The hunt and the chase supplied Hunter, Falconer, Fowler, Fox, Forrester, Archer and Spearman.

The renowned medieval historian Froissart, who eulogised about the romantic deeds of chivalry (and who condemned Scotland as being a poverty stricken wasteland), once sniffily dismissed the peasantry of his native France as the jacquerie (or the jacques-without-names) but it was these same humble folk who ended up overthrowing the arrogant aristocracy.

In the olden days, only the blueblooded knights of antiquity were entitled to full, proper names, both Christian and surnames, but with the passing of time and a more egalitarian, less feudal atmosphere, more respectful and worthy titles spread throughout the populace as a whole.

Echoes of a far distant past can still be found in most names and they can be borne with pride in commemoration of past generations who fought and toiled in some capacity or other to make our nation what it now is, for good or ill.

Chapter two:

In freedom's cause

Parts of Belgium, France, and the Netherlands now make up today what is known as the region of Flanders, and the surname Fleming stems from the Old French 'Flamanc', meaning a native of the area.

Flanders thrived for centuries as a great trading nation, particularly in fine linen and woollen cloth, and many of its subjects found a further outlet for their entrepreneurial skills by establishing trading colonies in other countries, including Scotland.

It was during the reign of King David I from 1124 until 1153 that Flemings, along with large numbers of Anglo-Norman adventurers, were encouraged to settle in Scotland, and over the centuries both groups formed an indissoluble bond with their adopted nation through intermarriage with the native Celtic stock.

David I had himself married a Flemish

princess, and the Flemings not only readily adapted to their new homeland but also acquired lands.

One of the main colonies of the Flemish settlers was in the Upper Clyde valley of Lanarkshire, and one family, descended from a Fleming known as Baldwin, acquired the lands of Biggar.

Another great influx of Flemings occurred from 1249 to 1286 during the reign of Alexander III, and it has been estimated that by the fourteenth century Flemings owned an impressive two thirds of Scottish trading vessels.

Many of these original natives of Flanders took the name of Fleming, and it was under this name that some were rewarded for their loyalty and service to the Scottish Crown with riches and honours.

Others took the name of the lands that had been granted to them by grateful monarchs, and it is because of this that Flemings of today can claim a kinship with Clan Murray.

This kinship is so strong that the Flemings are recognised as a sept, or branch, of this proud clan and therefore entitled to share in its rich heritage and traditions.

A Flemish nobleman known as Freskin, granted the lands of Strathbock, near Linlithgow, by David I, had rallied to his monarch's cause in 1130 to crush a rebellion against his royal authority by wild and unruly subjects in the northern Moray area of the kingdom.

As reward for his bravery, Freskin was granted lands in Moray. His descendants later took the name 'Moravia', or 'Moray', later anglicised as Murray.

The family flourished, giving rise to the principal branches of Tullibardine, Atholl, Abercairney, and Polmaise, and this explains why the Murrays of today can boast no less than three crests and accompanying mottos.

One of these crests features a naked savage firmly grasping a sword and a key, while the colourful motto is 'Furth Fortune and Fill the Fetters'.

This can be loosely translated as 'go forth against your enemies, enjoy good fortune, and return with rich plunder' – a motto that aptly describes the adventurous and martial spirit of the Murrays throughout Scotland's turbulent history.

Among the many glittering honours and titles acquired by the family over the generations are the Earldom of Tullibardine and the Earldom of Atholl, while the first Duke of Atholl was created in 1703.

Blair Atholl remains the family seat of the Dukes of Atholl, and it is the green Murray of Atholl tartan that Flemings of today who are recognised as having kinship with the Murrays are entitled to wear.

A family of Flemings who had settled in the Lowlands of Scotland also acquired honour and fame over the centuries.

Sir Malcolm Fleming was appointed sheriff of Dumbarton, on the west coast, and in the fifteenth century a descendant was honoured with the Earldom of Wigtown, in the southwest, followed later by the creation of the first Lord Fleming.

Both this family of Fleming and their Murray kinsfolk were destined to pay dearly for the riches and honours bestowed on them, not least through their support for the cause of Scotland's freedom during the bitter and bloody Wars of Independence with England.

The banner of revolt against the English occupation of Scotland was raised in May of 1297, after William Wallace slew Sir William Heselrig, Sheriff of Lanark, in revenge for the killing of his young wife, Marion.

Proving an expert in the tactics of guerrilla warfare, Wallace and his hardened band of freedom fighters inflicted stunning defeats on the English garrisons.

This culminated in the liberation of practically all of Scotland following the battle of Stirling Bridge, on September 11, 1297, a battle in which a young Sir Andrew Murray played a key role.

While Wallace had raised the south of

Scotland in revolt, Murray, who along with his father had been captured at the battle of Dunbar about a year earlier, sparked off the rising in the northeast.

The bold Murray managed to escape from his confinement in Chester Castle and, returning to his homelands and raising a force of loyal kinsmen and others who suffered under English occupation, captured the English held castles of Banff, Elgin, Inverness, and Urquhart.

The forces of Wallace and Murray met up and prepared to meet a mighty English invasion force that had been hurriedly despatched north by Edward I, known to posterity as the Hammer of the Scots.

Despite having a force of only thirty-six cavalry and 8,000 foot soldiers, compared to an army under the Earl of Surrey that boasted no less than 200 knights and 10,000 foot soldiers, the Scots held a strategic advantage that they exploited to the full.

Positioning their forces on the heights

of the Abbey Craig, on the outskirts of Stirling, and where the imposing Wallace Monument now stands, Wallace and Murray waited patiently as Essex's force slowly made its way across a narrow wooden bridge that spanned the waters of the Forth.

As the bulk of the English army crossed onto the marshy ground at the foot of the Abbey

Robert the Bruce, King of Scots   The Victor of Bannockburn

Craig, the piercing blast of a hunting horn signalled a ferocious charge down the hillside of massed ranks of Scottish spearmen.

Trapped on the boggy ground, the English were incapable of putting up any effective resistance.

They were hacked to death in their hundreds, while many others drowned in the fast-flowing waters of the Forth in their heavy armour as they attempted to make their way back across the narrow bridge.

Sir Andrew Murray had fought bravely, but tragically for Scotland he died in November from wounds he had received in the battle.

Sir Andrew's son, also Andrew, continued his father's struggle for Scotland's independence by fighting for the great warrior king Robert the Bruce at the battle of Bannockburn in 1314, and later married the king's sister, Christian.

Sir Robert Fleming, who also aided Bruce to victory at Bannockburn, was rewarded with lands forfeited from the powerful Comyns, including the barony of Cumbernauld.

Chapter three:

For the cause of Mary

Flemings and their Murray kinsfolk not only fought bravely in the cause of Scotland's freedom, but also in the bitter and destructive civil wars that wracked the nation and for the ultimately doomed cause of the Royal of Stuart.

Lord Fleming was among the 3,000 clansmen who formed part of the 35,000-strong Scots army that met a strategically superior English force at the battle of Pinkie, near Musselburgh, on Scotland's east coast, in September of 1547.

Fought during the infancy of Mary, Queen of Scots, the battle resulted in a resounding victory for the English invasion force and among the hundreds of dead who littered the battlefield was Lord Fleming.

Both his wife and daughter, however, were destined to become key figures in the tragic life and times of the ill-starred Mary who had inherited the troubled throne of Scotland when she was only one week old, following the death of her father, James V, on December 14, 1542.

With her mother, Mary of Guise, ruling as regent, Mary was sent for her own safety at the tender age of six to the French royal court.

Included in her entourage was her governess, Lady Fleming, the widow of the Lord Fleming who had fallen at the battle of Pinkie, and four young girls of the same age who also bore the name of Mary, or Marie.

These were the famous 'Four Marys': Mary Fleming, Mary Seton, Mary Beaton, and Mary Livingston.

All four of the young girls were the daughters of some of Scotland's noblest families but Mary Fleming, daughter of Lady Fleming, was considered particularly special because her mother was an illegitimate daughter of the queen's grandfather James IV.

Not commonly known is that the popular ballad *The Queen's Maries*, which suggests that

the Four Marys were Mary Carmichael, Mary
Hamilton, Mary Seaton, and Mary Beaton, was
originally based on a Mary Hamilton who was
involved in a scandal in the eighteenth century
court of Russia's Peter the Great!

'Mary' or 'Marie', meanwhile, stems
from the Icelandic word 'maer', meaning a virgin,
or a maid.

As the young queen and her four maids
settled into the opulent life of the French court,
Lady Fleming lost no time in attracting the
amorous eye of no less than the French monarch
himself, Henry II.

Eventually pregnant with his child,
embarrassed French and Scots courtiers had to
arrange for her return home to avoid further
scandal!

Mary married Francis, the French
Dauphin, in a magnificent ceremony in Notre
Dame Cathedral, in Paris, in April of 1558, just
over a year before her husband succeeded to the
throne following the death of his father.

By December of 1560, the young Mary

was widowed when the sickly Francis died, and she returned to Scotland to take up her throne in August of the following year.

By the time she returned, Scotland was in the uncompromising grip of a religious reformation whose stern adherents distrusted her Catholicism and frowned on the gaiety of her royal court.

This would result in a series of tragic events, including the murder of her Italian secretary, David Rizzio, the murder of her second husband, Lord Darnley, her enforced abdication in favour of her son, the future James VI, and her flight into exile and imprisonment in England.

It ended with her execution on February 8, 1587, in the Great Hall of Fotheringhay Castle, in Northamptonshire.

While her royal court in Edinburgh had sparkled under the refined French influences she had imported, it was Mary Fleming who was considered 'the flower of the flock' of her four loyal Marys.

Mary, who had inherited the fair Flemish

beauty of her mother, was courted by several important suitors, but eventually gave her hand in marriage to William Maitland of Lethington, the queen's powerful Secretary of State, on January 6, 1567.

Mary Seton, as the only unmarried one of the Four Marys, was the only one to accompany her mistress into her lonely exile in 1568.

Mary Fleming, however, right up until the queen's execution nearly twenty years later, remained loyal to her doomed cause.

Her husband, Maitland of Lethington, along with Sir William Kirkcaldy of Grange, successfully held the mighty bastion of Edinburgh Castle in the queen's name from April of 1571 until May of 1573.

Aided by English artillery, the Regent Morton bombarded the fortress and, realising the situation was hopeless, Kirkcaldy of Grange at last reluctantly agreed to its surrender.

He did not do so, however, before obtaining an assurance from the English commander that he and the surviving members of the garrison would be taken into their custody, rather than into that of the vengeful Morton.

The commander agreed, but the English later reneged on the deal, and Kirkcaldy of Grange was handed over to Morton.

Maitland had already died in prison, possibly by his own hand, but a much grimmer fate awaited Kirkcaldy, who was hanged at the Mercat Cross in Edinburgh on August 3.

His humiliation did not end with his death: following the barbaric custom of the time, his head was severed from his body and impaled for all to see on the walls of the very castle he and Maitland of Lethington had so nobly defended in the cause of their queen.

It was only through the impassioned pleas of Maitland's widow, Mary Fleming, that her husband's corpse was spared the same gruesome fate as that of Kirkcaldy of Grange.

Maitland's lands and possessions were forfeited, but Mary managed to have this reversed in 1583.

In later years, the Flemings and the

Murrays also found themselves at the heart of the divisive wars between Crown and Covenant.

A National Covenant had first been signed in the Greyfriars kirkyard, in Edinburgh, in February of 1638, pledging defence of the Presbyterian religion and defiance of Charles I's claim of supremacy in matters of religion.

Copies of the Covenant were circulated throughout the length and breadth of Scotland, and those who subscribed to it were known as Covenanters.

In the bitter civil war that followed the signing of the Covenant, the Murrays fought at the side of the Royalist John Graham, 1st Marquis of Montrose, during his campaigns in support of the king and in opposition to the Covenanters.

The 2nd Earl of Atholl, who had received Montrose at Blair Atholl in 1644, raised an impressive 1800 men for the royal cause.

The period from 1644-45 became known as the Year of Miracles because of Montrose's brilliant military successes.

These included the battle of Inverlochy, fought on February 2, 1645, when the Covenanting leader, the Earl of Argyll, was forced to flee to safety in his galley after 1,500 of his Covenanters were wiped out in a daring surprise attack.

What made Montrose's victory all the more remarkable was that his hardy band of men, including a contingent of Athollmen, had arrived at Inverlochy after enduring a gruelling thirty-six hour march through knee-deep snow from the area of present-day Fort Augustus to Inverlochy.

The Athollmen also shared in Montrose's victory at Kilsyth on August 15, 1645, but also in his final defeat at Philiphaugh, near Selkirk, less than a month later.

Flemings, through their kinship with the Murrays, were also at the forefront of the Jacobite Risings of 1715, 1719, and 1745.

They are particularly associated with the Rising of 1745 in the form of Lord George Murray, the Lieutenant General of the Jacobite Army who, following the disastrous defeat of

Prince Charles Stuart at the battle of Culloden on
Drummossie Moor, near Inverness, in April 1746,
died in exile in Holland fourteen years later.

Chapter four:

On the world stage

Far from the battlefield, generations of Flemings have achieved distinction in a number of rather more peaceful pursuits, not least Sir Alexander Fleming, who discovered the antibiotic known as penicillin.

Born on a farm at Lochiel, near Darvel, in Ayrshire, in 1881, Fleming studied as a biologist and pharmacologist and was the first to isolate penicillin from a fungus.

Two other scientists, Howard Florey and Ernst Chain, were able to develop a method of purifying the antibiotic, and for this important work all three shared the 1945 Nobel Prize in Medicine.

During the Second World War, Fleming was responsible for saving the life of the British war time leader Winston Churchill, who had taken seriously ill while on a visit to North Africa, by flying to him with a batch of the rare penicillin.

The antibiotic also saved the lives of countless wounded military personnel throughout the course of the conflict.

Knighted in 1944, Fleming was accorded the status of a British national hero on his death in 1955 when he was interred in a crypt in St. Paul's Cathedral, in London.

Also in the scientific field, Sir John Ambrose Fleming, born in 1849, was the English physicist and electrical engineer whose invention of the radio valve in 1904 paved the way for radio broadcasting and television.

Ian Fleming, born in London in 1908 and who died in 1964, was the former officer with British Naval Intelligence during the Second World War who penned the hugely popular series of James Bond spy novels, in addition to the children's book *Chitty Chitty Bang Bang*.

His first novel featuring James Bond, 007, was *Casino Royale*, published in 1953, while a string of successful film adaptations of his books began in 1961 with *Dr. No*.

Fleming originally suggested his cousin,

the actor Christopher Lee, for the role of Bond. Lee was never given the role, but he played a memorable villain in the Bond film *The Man with the Golden Gun*.

Also in the world of film Victor Fleming, better known as Vic Fleming, born in 1883 and who died in 1949, was the American film director whose many film credits include *Gone With The Wind* and *The Wizard of Oz*.

In contemporary times, Stephen Fleming, born in Christchurch, New Zealand, in 1973 is the talented left-handed batsman who, at the time of writing, is captain of both the New Zealand Cricket Team and Nottinghamshire County Cricket Club.